D0893558

Like us on
Facebook

ROLE-PLAYING FOR FUN AND PROFIT™

THEME PARKS

BOBI MARTIN

rosen publishing's
rosen
central®
New York

Published in 2016 by The Rosen Publishing Group, Inc.
29 East 21st Street, New York, NY 10010

Copyright © 2016 by The Rosen Publishing Group, Inc.

First Edition

Library of Congress Cataloging-in-Publication Data

Martin, Bobi.
Theme parks / Bobi Martin.
  pages cm
Includes bibliographical references and index.
ISBN 978-1-4994-3734-8 (library bound) — ISBN 978-1-4994-3732-4 (pbk.) — ISBN 978-1-4994-3733-1 (6-pack)
1. Amusement parks—Juvenile literature. 2. Role playing—Juvenile literature I. Title.
GV1851.M37 2016
791.06'8—dc23

2015022710

Manufactured in the United States of America

INTRODUCTION

Costumed characters help bring a park's theme to life. This costume Megatron from the *Transformers* movies welcomes guests to the Transformers ride at Universal Studios in Hollywood, California.

What could be more fun than going to a theme park? Getting paid to be there! There are hundreds of amusement and theme parks across the United States and Canada, and all of them hire teens to work for them.

Theme parks are designed around a particular story, idea or set of characters. For example, the attractions and costumed characters in Disneyland are based on Disney productions. Park guests can meet the iconic Mickey Mouse, as well as characters such as Anna and Buzz Lightyear from the popular animated films *Frozen* and *Toy Story*, respectively. Many of the characters at Universal parks appear in movies or programs produced by Universal Studios, including the Minions from the *Despicable Me* franchise. Others, such as Scooby-Doo, SpongeBob SquarePants, Shrek, and, in Orlando, Marvel superheroes, are characters from studios or parties with which Universal has a licensing agreement.

Characters bring a park's theme to life, especially for the youngest park visitors who may think they are meeting the "real" character from their favorite movie. This is great news for teens, since most theme parks depend on teens to fill the need for costumed characters.

Teens are needed for other roles, too. Parks hire teens to escort costumed characters from the dressing area to the area where the character is to meet the public. Most costumed characters are not allowed to talk, so escorts help answer questions children ask the characters and keep anxious or excited guests from mobbing the character.

A number of parks also hire teens to sing, dance, or perform onstage. Some teens may prefer a position backstage where they help create costumes or assist with makeup. Other teens take jobs building the sets and props used for performances. Most amusement and theme parks also hire teens to work in concession stands, gift shops, and ticket booths or as lifeguards at pools or lazy rivers. Older teens may be ride operators.

Besides earning a paycheck and getting to see what goes on behind the scenes, there are other fun benefits to working at a theme park. Many parks host one or more employee-only events each year during which employees get to try out all the rides. Some parks also plan fun outings for their seasonal workers. Employees are usually given some free tickets to share with family or friends. Older teens may take advantage of one of the summer exchange programs that allows them to work at a theme park in another country.

Best of all, the skills teens learn while working at a theme park can lead to a number of careers later on. Frank Oznowicz (better known as Frank Oz) had fun as a teen while working on the puppet shows at Fairyland, a small theme park in Oakland, California. He used that experience later to work on the popular television shows *Sesame Street* and *The Muppet Show*.

From an onstage role as an actor, singer, or dancer to an escort or a costumed character, there are many ways to role-play at a theme park. If you like being outdoors and enjoy helping people have a good time, stepping into the role of a costumed character or other theme park worker could be your ticket to the best summer job ever.

CHAPTER ONE

GETTING PAID TO HAM IT UP

Being a costumed character at an amusement park or theme park can make a summer job seem more like play than work. Characters get to interact with guests of all ages and are actually encouraged to ham it up a bit! Costumed characters are divided into two categories: fur characters and face characters. The "fur" category includes any character that has a costume that hides the wearer's whole body and face, whether the actual costume has fur or not. So, when someone is in a full-body costume as a character, such as SpongeBob SquarePants or Woody from *Toy Story*, he or she would be a fur character. At some parks, these characters may be called fuzzies, cartoon characters, or mascots.

No matter what the character is called, teens with a lot of energy and enthusiasm do well in costume. Costumed characters need to be able to move about and bend down to hug small children. Sometimes they may be asked to dance a little or to walk in parades.

A large part of the job involves greeting guests and posing for pictures. A highlight of this position is watching children's faces

Adults and kids alike love posing with costumed characters! These Minion characters from the *Despicable Me* movies are considered "fur" characters, even though the costumes are not furry.

light up with delight when they get to hug, shake hands with, or have their picture taken with a favorite character. At the same time, some children may become suddenly fearful, so costumed characters sometimes need to move slowly or even back away and give a child time to feel comfortable with them. Whether a child is excited or shy, it is important to remember that many young children believe costumed characters are real. The experience they have when meeting their favorite character is important to their parents—which means it is also important to the theme park.

To help fur characters with their role, most parks hire character escorts. Escorts help characters get from backstage costuming to the spot where they will be meeting guests. And since escorts can talk, they help answer questions guests ask the characters. Escorts also help keep children and their parents from rushing a character all at once.

PERFORMING FOR OTHERS

Face characters wear costumes, too, but their heads are not covered. Face characters at Universal parks include Shaggy from Scooby-Doo and Princess Fiona from *Shrek*. At Disney parks, any of the Disney princesses are examples of face characters. Face characters talk with guests, pose for pictures, and

Face characters such as Princess Fiona from the *Shrek* movies are able to talk with guests and enjoy more freedom of movement than characters with full-body costumes.

sign autographs. Like fur or cartoon characters, a face character should have good energy and enthusiasm and should enjoy working with children. Because these positions have a larger degree of performance involved, an actor needs to know his or her character and the movie the character is featured in to the smallest detail. Staying true to the character a performer is portraying is vital because it helps preserve the magic for child guests.

Theme parks also provide live shows or other entertainment. Teens who can sing, dance, or act may enjoy participating in these performances. Amusement parks and some theme parks, such as Silverwood, in Idaho, may also look for specialty performers such as jugglers or magicians to wander through the park, interacting with guests on a more casual basis. Legoland in California hires teens to be guest experience hosts. These performers lead guests through a live soundstage, sharing information about *The LEGO Movie*, guiding the guests through scavenger hunt games, and answering questions.

MAKING IT LOOK FUN TAKES HARD WORK

A good actor makes it look easy to play the part, but like anything else, performing takes practice and has challenges. For example, it can get very hot inside a costume, so fur characters who work outside in the sun must drink lots of water to stay hydrated. They are often limited to thirty minutes of guest interaction at one time and are then given a break to cool off before going out again. But they may go out four or more times in one day. Other times, characters are stationed in a shaded place or meet guests at an indoor location. Characters need to show a lot of enthusiasm, even at the end of their appearance when they may be hot and tired.

Another challenge is that fur or mascot characters are not allowed to talk. Instead, actors learn to use pantomime skills, gesturing with their characters' hands and bodies to communicate. It is hard to see well inside a costume, and it can be tricky to maneuver a bulky costume, so costumed characters must be careful when moving to avoid bumping into people or objects. Characters also have to learn to deal with guests that are not well behaved. Some kids may hit or kick characters to get their attention. A tired or frightened child may scream, cry, or throw a tantrum. Costumed characters have to keep their cool—and their silence—even at times like these. They learn to work with their escort to remove themselves from the area if necessary.

Although they are not in a costume, escorts play an important role. They are responsible for helping guests have a positive experience, while also assisting characters. Besides helping a costumed character navigate safely through crowds, an escort helps protect the character from unruly guests who pull or tug at his or her costume. Escorts sometimes have to ask parents to help their child wait for his or her turn to be photographed with the character, or they may have to tell children not to pull on the character's costume without upsetting the children's parents. They have to keep their composure when tired or frazzled parents get angry about waiting for their child's turn to meet the character.

Seasoned performers never let the audience know if a mistake has been made during a show. Keeping their cool allows them to retain the magic of a character.

Escorts also learn how to answer questions directed at the character in a way that lets children feel as if the character answered the question. And escorts learn to read signals from a character indicating that he or she is too hot or needs to use the restroom.

Face characters learn how to do the proper makeup for their characters and learn how to put on their wigs, costumes, and any accessories. They usually spend several days in training learning how to be the character they are portraying. This is

SOMETIMES SIZE MATTERS

Experience in performing before a crowd can be helpful in landing a job as a costumed character, but a person's height is an important factor, too. Cartoon character costumes generally fall into a shorter height range. For example, at both Knott's Berry Farm, in California, and at Canada's Wonderland, an amusement park in Toronto, Ontario, costumed characters must be between 4'7" (1.4 meters) and 5'3" (1.6 m) tall. Cedar Point, in Ohio, needs performers from 4'6" (1.37 m) to 5'2" (1.57 m) for its costumed characters. At Universal parks, the height requirements range from 3'6" (1.07 m) to more than 6' (1.83 m) tall! Like Universal, some other parks have taller characters. For its Garfield and Odie costumed characters, Silverwood, in Idaho, looks for performers up to 5'7" (1.7 m) tall, and Legoland parks in California and Florida want performers from 5'4" (1.63 m) to 5'7" (1.7 m) for their costumed character roles.

important since some guests quiz characters to see if they can catch them in an error. Young children may want a costumed character to do something he or she did in a movie, such as fly or speak another language. Face characters learn to improvise, or quickly make up, responses to new questions. Many have memorized a few answers for frequent questions.

Singers, actors, and dancers rehearse their shows, but sometimes problems happen during a performance. Someone may forget a line, or a prop might not work or may not be in the right place. Sound equipment may not work correctly, or a rude person in the audience may shout insults at the performers.

Participating in band, choir, or drama club or acting in a school play or annual talent show all count as performing experience.

Good performers learn to keep their cool and finish the show as if nothing has happened.

GETTING EXPERIENCE

Many parks prefer teens aged sixteen and older for performing roles, while others hire students as young as fourteen and fifteen. But would-be performers can start getting experience even before they are old enough to apply for a job. Participating in band, choir, or drama club or being in the school's annual talent show or school play counts as performing experience. Many communities have a local theater group that puts on several productions a year, and dance schools hold recitals. All of these count as performing experience, as well.

Temporary jobs and volunteering count, too. Local businesses sometimes hire young teens on a short-term basis to wear a costume and hold a large sign outside their building to attract business. Some schools look for one or more students to wear the school mascot costume at pep rallies and sporting events. Working in ticket sales, at a food or game booth at a school's carnival, or at a local fair are good ways to get experience working with the public. Babysitting, being a summer camp counselor, or being a lifeguard at a local pool are other good ways to get experience in working with younger children.

OTHER ROLES AT THEME PARKS

What if being a performer is not in your comfort zone but you still want to work at a theme park? No problem! It takes a lot of people to run a busy park, and there are many other roles that parks need to fill. Some involve guest relations and allow you to interact with park visitors without putting on a costume. Others work behind the scenes to help make staged performances and attractions possible. All help keep a park running smoothly.

PARK OPERATIONS AND GUEST SERVICES

Teens who don't want to be entertainers but like working with the public may enjoy being at the front gates as a ticket seller. A cheerful smile and the ability to handle transactions quickly to keep the lines moving are good assets for this position. Good math skills are important as well. Others may like working in guest relations answering questions, assisting with stroller or wheelchair rentals, or helping to resolve problems or concerns guests may have.

Some parks, such as Dorney Park in Pennsylvania, hire teens to be tour guides.

Teens who show that they can work with limited supervision may work at one of the various food or beverage carts throughout the park. Some parks hire teens to be hosts or hostesses at one of their restaurants. There are also positions as servers, bussers, and dishwashers.

Many parks also need cheerful, friendly teens to run game booths. Teens in this position should be outgoing and must enjoy interacting with people of all ages. Game booth attendants need to persuade passing guests to try their game, explain how the

Many parks look for outgoing teens to run game booths. Teens in this position should like interacting with guests of all ages.

game is played, and award prizes. They may also be responsible for assisting with inventory of the prizes and for keeping their area clean and attractive.

And what is a trip to a theme park without a souvenir? Most parks have several gift shops and need a number of helpful people to staff them. Photographs make good souvenirs, and digital cameras make taking great photos simple. An increasing number of parks, from Stone Mountain Park in Georgia to Splish Splash Water Park in New York to Knott's Berry Farm in California, are looking for people with friendly personalities to photograph families as they enter the park or to work at a special photo station that is set up with fun props. Amusement parks may also hire teens to assist with sales of the candid photos taken on some thrill rides.

Some parks, such as Playland in Vancouver, Canada, have a petting zoo and need attendants who are comfortable working with animals. Duties there may include teaching children how to approach animals correctly, answering questions about different types of animals, cleaning up the area to keep it sanitary, and helping groom and feed the animals. Parks with water play areas such as wave pools and lazy rivers need many lifeguards, and parks that have arts and crafts areas need teens that like to help young guests make creative souvenirs.

WORKING BEHIND THE SCENES

For those who like being part of performances without being onstage, there are a number of supporting roles. Ushers are needed to help seat people before shows and to help them

IS IT AN AMUSEMENT PARK OR A THEME PARK?

Both theme parks and amusement parks have a variety of rides for kids and adults. Both usually have staged shows and other entertainment, as well as concession stands and restaurants. So how are they different?

Theme parks are designed around a particular idea. The rides, shows, buildings, and even food choices tie into a specific theme. For example, the theme of Dollywood, in Tennessee, revolves around the traditions and family values of the southern Appalachian area. Disney parks are themed around Disney productions. Like many large theme parks, Disneyland in California is divided into several areas with different, but connected, themes such as Fantasyland, Frontierland, and so on. The rides, buildings, and restaurants in each land tie into that particular land's theme with Disney movies and characters connecting all of the lands to the park's overall theme.

An amusement park has no theme. It is more like a giant carnival that is permanently placed. The big draw of an amusement park is its thrill rides. For example, Cedar Point Amusement Park, along Lake Erie, has a beach area and a water park with many attractions. It also has an amazing collection of roller coasters, such as Top Thrill Dragster—one of the fastest and tallest roller coasters in the world. There may even be costumed characters, but there is no specific theme that ties everything together. A theme park is generally considered a type of amusement park, but amusement parks are not always theme parks.

exit when the show is over. They may also need to assist guests with disabilities or answer questions about the performance. Backstage roles include positions in the wardrobe or costuming department. Beginning duties here may involve checking costumes out to performers, helping actors with quick changes during a performance, and assisting with fittings, cleaning, or repairs.

Universal theme parks list positions such as entertainment coordinators, makeup artists, assistant stage managers, and administrative assistants among their backstage support roles. Some parks have seasonal positions working with the lighting

Backstage support roles, such as entertainment coordinators, assistant stage mangers, wardrobe, hairdressers, and makeup artists, are all important to the success of every performance.

and sound crew, with the backstage crew, or as a stage technician. Artistic teens might look for a position in set design. Those with computer experience might look into video programming positions. Older teens that have experience working with power tools may be hired to help build sets and props. Experience is a definite plus in getting hired, but amusement and theme park companies know that they may be providing a teen's first job. They want all employees to succeed and will provide training for each position. A few jobs may require specialized training or certification. For example, lifeguards generally are required to have cardiopulmonary resuscitation (CPR) certification before they are hired.

Repeat Performances

Many teens who work at a theme park return year after year. Some return to the same department, working their way into positions with more responsibility and a better paycheck. A singer or dancer who was in the chorus last season has gained experience that might help him or her land a supporting or leading role this time. Or he or she may be asked to perform multiple parts.

A teen starting out in a gift shop might do mostly shelving and stocking one season, work primarily as a sales clerk the next year, and eventually work his or her way up to being a supervisor or an assistant manager. A ride attendant assists with crowd control, ensures young children meet the height restriction for the ride, and assists with cleaning the ride units. This position can lead to a role as a ride operator, which entails responsibility for inspecting and running the ride and making sure safety restraints are properly used.

Working in the restaurant area provides multiple opportunities for advancement. Hosts, hostesses, and bussers can become servers. Servers may be asked to help at special catering events or VIP parties for important guests.

Some parks, such as Canada's Wonderland, offer management opportunities and management training programs for their seasonal employees who want to advance with the company. Wild Adventures Theme Park, located in Georgia, posts several possible career paths on its website to show how seasonal, part-time employees can advance their careers there.

Some teens who return to the same park each summer prefer to try out different areas each year. This is a smart strategy.

Ride operators are responsible for inspecting and running a ride. They also make sure safety restraints are in good condition and are properly used.

A number of theme park jobs can lead to well-paying career paths. Working in different areas of the park each year is a great way for a teen to sample different career possibilities to see which one is the best fit before heading off to a technical school or college.

EDUCATIONAL SUPPORT

While theme parks know the value of play and recreation, they also value education—so much so that another benefit of working for a park is that many of them assist their employees with college costs. For example, the Dollywood parks in Tennessee, Kings Island in Ohio, and Calaway Amusement Park in Alberta, Canada, are just a few of the parks that offer scholarship opportunities. Disney parks, Six Flags, and Cedar Point are among those that offer college students internship positions. And nearly all parks offer flexible scheduling that enables students to attend classes and work at the same time.

Theme park companies realize that employees who like what they are doing will do a better job than unhappy employees. And happy employees mean happy guests!

CHAPTER THREE

YOUR HAPPY EVER AFTER

While amusement parks in states with very cold winters tend to close at the end of summer, parks in areas with mild weather generally remain open on the weekends all year. These parks are usually also open weekdays during major school holidays, such as winter and spring breaks. Major parks such as Universal and Disney World remain open all year.

Whether they are open year-round or just for the summer, many amusement and theme parks need full-time employees as well as the teens and college students who work only during the summer season. And that means that seasonal employees who want to turn their summer job into a full-time career after they finish high school or college already have a foot in the door.

BUILDING A THEME PARK CAREER

Most companies like to promote from within, and amusement and theme parks are no exception. For example, someone who worked as a costumed character could advance to become a trainer and then a training coordinator who works with escorts and characters. Some parks have an entertainment team lead. This position supervises performers, theater staff, and costumed characters, among others. From there he or she could advance to become an entertainment supervisor or a department manager. A different avenue for a costumed character could be in the wardrobe and costume department. In this position, someone with sewing experience might become a stitcher. Stitchers sew new costumes to replace those that are wearing out and repair costumes with minor damage. A fur character

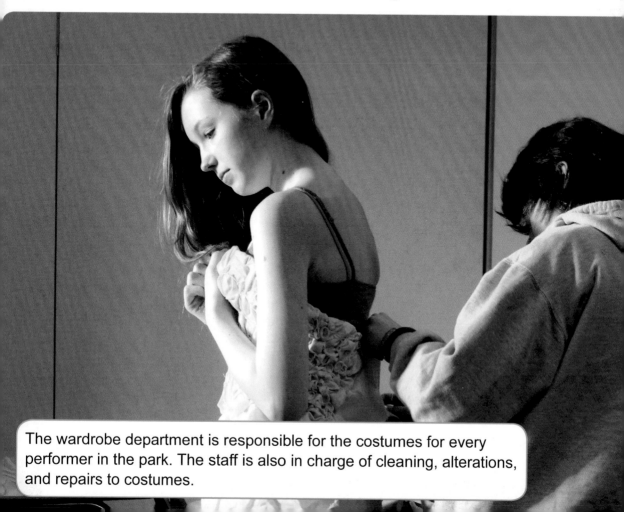

The wardrobe department is responsible for the costumes for every performer in the park. The staff is also in charge of cleaning, alterations, and repairs to costumes.

moving into this area might use his or her experience inside the costume to design improvements to existing costumes.

Those who start in the costume and wardrobe department have many options as well. As new characters are introduced, new costumes have to be designed and created. Wardrobes also have to be created for the singers, dancers, and actors who perform onstage at the park. And since shows change from year to year, wardrobes must change with them. Promotions within this department could include becoming a costume designer, a supervisor in the wardrobe or costuming department, or the head of the department.

A dancer may go on to become a dance captain, or he or she may become a choreographer who plans the dance moves for performances.

Singers, dancers, and stage actors move from smaller roles to supporting or starring roles. An actor could also become a stage manager—the person who oversees all behind-the-scenes activity during a production. Or such a performer may become a casting director who holds auditions and casts people for performances or even the director of the production. Dancers may go on to become dance captains, or they may become choreographers who plan the dance moves for each scene.

Those who work in ticket sales, gift shops, or other customer service positions might advance as supervisors, assistant managers, or department managers. People who like training others might move into the human resources department where they assist with recruiting and hiring employees, holding training sessions, explaining benefits, and resolving problems. Those who love working on the rides could become supervisors over the employees of one or several rides. A different move would be going into the maintenance department. Maintenance is responsible for testing every ride every day, for maintaining and repairing every ride and attraction in the park, and for maintaining other buildings and structures in the park.

A person in photo operations can move up from photographer to a team lead position. Team leads usually perform some of the same duties as photographers, while also supervising other workers in their department. A lead may also be responsible for making and filing reports to the department head.

Positions in restaurants at theme parks can lead to jobs with a park's catering department. The catering team prepares and serves meals at special events and promotions. They may also be responsible for creating special displays and elaborate decorations for special events.

A Ticket to a New Career

Almost all jobs at theme parks make great stepping-stones to careers in other areas. For example, those who worked as ride operators might become equipment operators in a factory. Those who moved into the maintenance department might work in the maintenance department in any number of industries. Or they can enter the engineering field to work on designing or improving rides.

Working in the costume and wardrobe department of a theme park could lead to a similar position with a television or movie company or with a clothing manufacturer. Someone with a degree in business might open his or her own costume rental shop. And someone with a driving passion for this area might go on to study fashion and become a designer.

Actors, singers, and dancers may use their theme park performances to land roles in local or regional theaters. Those looking to reach wider audiences may aspire to commercial, movie, or television roles. Or they may perform in Broadway shows. Those with good speaking voices may become radio or television announcers or do voice-overs. Actors who also like writing may become scriptwriters or screenwriters.

Artistic people who work backstage may become set designers, creating the backgrounds and settings for theater, television, or movie productions. A stagehand who assists the stage manager may become a property master—the person in

charge of developing or obtaining props used in various performances. Those who work with the lighting or sound departments
at a theme park may pursue careers as lighting or sound engineers in the movie or television industry. Teens and young adults
who work in gift shops may pursue a business degree and own
their own business. Or, they may go into product design, creating
new items that people want to buy.

Positions with a park's restaurant or catering department
are great stepping-stones for those who want to pursue a career
in catering, restaurant or event management, or the tourism
industry. Teens who work in the photo operations area of a

Those who work in the lighting or sound departments of a theme park
may go on to become lighting or sound engineers in the entertainment
industry.

park might pursue careers as professional photographers with a newspaper or magazine publisher. They might work in the corporate communications department of a large firm or work for a publicity agency. Or they could become freelance photographers or videographers who photograph or film weddings, baptisms, birthdays, anniversaries, and other special events.

Teens looking to get into other career areas can also point to their theme park experience. Those working as costumed characters or in guest services positions can highlight their ability to work with a wide variety of people, a quality many employers in many fields find attractive. Performance experience can also be

Whether they want to freelance or work for a company, teens can use their theme park photography experience to become professional photographers or videographers.

useful in any position that requires presenting in front of others or interacting with different types of clients. Management positions in a gift shop, restaurant, or other theme park department will demonstrate experience supervising a staff. Whatever field

A CHANCE TO SEE THE WORLD

David Duncan was applying for a position at Walt Disney World in Florida when something even better caught his attention. Disney Cruise Lines was looking for a youth activities counselor. "The opportunity to travel and work with kids really appealed to me," says Duncan. His previous experience as a summer camp counselor helped him land the job.

As a youth activities director, Duncan entertained children of different ages with a variety of fun activities and programs. His team also put together activities built around visits by costumed characters. "We had programs like Pluto's Pajama Party and Cinderella's Ball."

Duncan says his experience with the theme ship helped him when he applied for teaching positions later. "The fact that I regularly worked with 200 or more kids at a time showed management skills, creativity, and flexibility."

In the four years he worked with Disney Cruise Line, Duncan was able to visit eleven countries and territories, including Aruba, St. Thomas, the Bahamas, and Canada. "Having the opportunity to see so many different sights, all while working with hundreds of kids, has been one of the most rewarding—and life changing—experiences of my life," he says.

you choose, there are many ways your theme park experience can serve you in the future.

Exchange Programs

Older teens and young adults can use their work experience at a local amusement or theme park to land an opportunity to work in a park in another country. Many countries, such as the United States, Canada, and Australia, have exchange programs that allow young people to live in their country while working at a theme park.

Through its Work and Travel Program (WAT), Janus International helps college students find positions at amusement parks and resorts around the world. After graduating college, students who have participated in a WAT program may apply for an internship. World Wide Cultural Exchange (WWCE) also has an exchange program and an internship program. Some companies, such as Disney, which has theme parks in several countries, have their own exchange programs. Fringe benefits vary depending on the company and the country. Some programs provide housing and discounted meals, while others assist workers in finding low-cost housing.

Whether you want to stay close to home or find a way to get paid while traveling around the world, theme parks have a lot to offer. Some workers will stay in the same department, while others may sample several areas before finding the job that suits them best.

CHAPTER FOUR

GETTING READY FOR YOUR CLOSE-U

That old saying "the early bird gets the worm" definitely applies when it comes to finding a job with a theme park. Savvy job hunters start looking well before the last week of school. Many parks start filling their seasonal positions in April and May, and some parks start their summer hiring process in January! This is particularly true for positions that require auditions, such as stage performers and costumed character positions.

FINDING JOB OPENINGS

While some parks place job advertisements in local newspapers, the fastest way to find out about job openings at theme parks is often online. Almost all amusement and theme parks have a website. These sites are easily found by typing the name of the theme park into a search engine. Some parks also have a Facebook page on which they list their website.

Most parks have a link at the bottom of their home page for "jobs" or "careers." On the jobs page, there is usually a

Since almost all amusement and theme parks have a website, the fastest way to find job openings at a park is often online.

brief description of the duties of each position. Many parks also list the minimum age a person must be to apply for that job. If the position requires an audition, information about that will be noted as well. Universal has a Twitter account for entertainers who want to follow their audition schedule. Some sites will also have a frequently asked questions (FAQ) link. Reading through these questions and responses can help answer some questions first-time job hunters may have. A growing number of parks invite job seekers to complete an online application and attach a résumé, while some companies still prefer that applicants complete a paper application. Paper applications should be neatly filled out in blue or black pen. An application that is messy or difficult to read may be set aside or tossed.

CREATING A RÉSUMÉ

Along with filling out an application form, job hunters may also be asked to provide a résumé. For teens with little or no job experience, the idea of creating a résumé can seem daunting, but it is actually a great help in getting an interview. A résumé is a job hunter's opportunity to tell future employers about him- or herself. This is a document that lists skills or describes experience that a job application may not have space for.

For most teens, a résumé will be only one page long. It should be typed in a clean, simple font such as Times New Roman, Calibri, or Arial, using a size 12 font. Avoid using large type or fancy fonts, as this is unprofessional. Have an adult proofread the résumé for spelling, grammar, and punctuation errors. A simple format on plain white paper is fine. Most public libraries have books on creating résumés that show a variety of templates, or formats. Free résumé templates can also be found online through a basic web search.

At the top of the résumé, job hunters should list their name, street address, phone number, and e-mail address. Drop down a few lines and list any work or volunteer experience, job skills, and education. Work experience can include mowing lawns, babysitting, or selling items for a school or club fund-raiser. Even if no actual paycheck was involved, these kinds of positions show responsibility, as well as an ability to follow directions and complete a task. Volunteer experiences such as working at a school carnival, helping at a local food bank, or participating in an after-school club can also be listed on a résumé.

Under education, teens should list their current grade and the name of their current school. Be sure to mention participation in marching band, glee club, or other school activities. This shows performing experience and demonstrates an ability to work with others. List any awards. For example, perfect attendance shows dependability. Job skills include the ability to use common word-processing and spreadsheet applications, good math or money-handling skills, and typing speed. Teens applying for an entertainment position should list performances in

Teens applying to be performers should mention any singing, dancing, or acting skills they have, as well as any instruments they play well.

school plays or local theaters, any instruments they play well, or singing, dancing, or acting skills. For backstage positions, teens should list sewing skills or any set or costume design experience they may have.

INTERVIEW DOS AND DON'TS

Here are a few tips hiring managers often recommend for a successful interview experience:

- Be polite to everyone around you. This includes other job applicants and the receptionist. While you are waiting for your interview, the employment staff is watching how you treat people to see how you will treat their guests.
- Dress nicely. This means slacks or khakis and a nice shirt for boys and slacks or skirts with a sweater or blouse or dresses for girls. Wear appropriate shoes—avoid tennis shoes, flip-flops, and other casual footwear.
- Avoid clothes that are too tight or too baggy. Girls should avoid low-cut or see-through tops and tops with spaghetti straps.
- Use proper grammar and avoid slang and profanity.
- Turn off your cell phone and leave it in your pocket or purse during the interview.
- Do not bring food or a beverage to the interview. Do not chew gum or suck on a piece of candy.
- Never criticize or run down a past employer or coworker. This leaves interviewers with a bad impression of you.
- Remember to smile and to thank the interviewer for his or her time. Polite manners leave a good impression.

Preparing for an Interview

Almost everyone feels nervous when he or she goes to an interview. Practicing with an adult ahead of time will help build confidence. Rehearse walking into the room with a smile and looking at the interviewer's face while shaking hands. This helps create a positive first impression. Practice sitting up straight and answering questions in a calm, clear voice.

Know something about the theme park. Many times interviewers ask a few questions to see what the job seeker knows about their company. It is OK to mention previous visits or a favorite ride or memory at the park. It is also OK to mention having read the job description on the company's website. At the end of an interview, hiring managers typically ask if the job seeker has any questions. This is not the time to ask questions about money, time off, or job perks. Instead, ask such questions as: What are you looking for in your ideal person for this job? Are there opportunities to move up in this position? When do you think you will be making a hiring decision?

Last, it is also a good idea to rehearse standing at the end of the interview and thanking the interviewer for his or her time. Don't be afraid to ask for the job. A simple, "Thank you for meeting with me. I would love to work here!" shows interest in the position.

Auditioning

Entertainment positions require an audition, or tryout. Auditions differ from one park to another, depending on the part to be filled. Some parks, like Calaway Park in Alberta, Canada, hold open auditions where all participants arrive at the same time. Others, like Legoland in California, hold auditions by appointment. Most parks describe their audition process on their website or provide a number to call for more information.

Different kinds of auditions will require different types of preparation. Generally, singers are asked to bring sheet music or a CD for two or more songs and be prepared to sing a certain number of bars of each song. Dancers may be asked to come prepared with a short dance routine, or they may be taught a

Dancers may be asked to audition privately, or they may be shown a short routine in a group setting and then audition with other dancers.

combination of steps in a group setting and then audition with other dancers. They should pay attention to the clothing requirements listed in the posting, as they should be able to move comfortably. As with an interview, audition clothing should be clean and not distracting in any way. Those looking to become a costumed character usually audition by putting on a costume provided by the park and then showing their ability to interact and communicate with guests through body movements. They may also be asked to demonstrate their ability to bend, walk, or shake hands or to do a few simple dance steps. Actors might be asked to read from a script or do a short improvised bit. No matter what part a person is auditioning for, a résumé and a head shot (a close-up photograph of the person's head) should be taken to the audition.

Sometimes hiring decisions are made at the audition, but often people are notified later if they got the part. Some people may be asked for a callback, which means they are invited to come back for a second audition before a decision is made.

Some teens will shine in the spotlight, while others will flourish in a backstage role. Some will work at a theme park just for a fun summer job, while some will use their theme park experience as a stepping-stone to a career in or out of a theme park. No matter what role you are interested in, working at a theme park makes a great way to spend a summer.

audition To try out for a part in a performance by acting, singing, or dancing; also, the act of trying out.

backstage Areas of a theater or performance area not visible to an audience during a staged performance.

callback An invitation for a second opportunity to audition.

candid Unplanned; a photograph in which people do not pose.

choreographer A person who designs and directs dance movements in a performance.

concession stand A small stand where people can buy snacks.

engineer A person who designs or creates something, often using math and scientific knowledge.

head shot A professional photograph of a person's face or face and shoulders only.

improvise Quickly invent or substitute an answer or action.

internship A usually temporary position that can be paid or unpaid and that gives young workers professional experience and training in a particular field.

inventory A complete account or list of items in a place.

pantomime Communication that relies on gestures rather than talking in order to convey information.

résumé A document that provides an overview or summary of a person's work experience, skills, and education.

soundstage A soundproof room or studio where TV or movie scenes are filmed.

template A document that serves as an example of how other documents should be formatted.

VIP Short for a very important person.

Canada's Wonderland
9580 Jane Street
Vaughan, ON L6A 1S6
Canada
Website: http://www.canadaswonderland.com
One of Canada's largest amusement and water parks, Canada's
　　Wonderland offers many different employment opportunities
　　for teens.

Janus International
16102 Theme Park Way
Doswell, VA 23407
(866) 249-3888
Website: http://www.janus-international.com
Janis International works with multiple theme parks, national
　　parks, hotels, and resorts to provide cultural exchange and
　　internship programs for college students interested in working
　　as seasonal employees.

Pacific National Exhibition (PNE)
2901 East Hastings Street
Vancouver, BC V5K 5J1
Canada
Website: http://www.pne.ca
The largest youth employer in British Columbia, the PNE hosts an
　　annual summer fair. It is also the site of Playland Amusement
　　Park.

Walt Disney World Resort
Orlando, FL 32830
(407) 939-5277
Website: disneyworld.disney.go.com
One of several Disney theme parks, Disney World has multiple
parks on this site including Epcot, Disney's Animal King-
dom, Disney's Hollywood Studios, and various themed hotel
resorts.

Young Actors Guild (YAG)
110 8th Street
Troy, NY 12180
(518) 276-2364
Website: http://yag.union.rpi.edu
YAG is one of the longest-running children's theaters in upstate
New York. YAG provides theater arts training, summer
camps, high school apprenticeships, and college internship
programs.

WEBSITES

Because of the changing nature of Internet links, Rosen Publishing has developed an online list of websites related to the subject of this book. This site is updated regularly. Please use this link to access this list:

http://www.rosenlinks.com/RPFP/Parks

Clavé, S. Anton. *The Global Theme Park Industry*. Cambridge, MA: CABI, 2007.

Donahue, Tim, and Jim Patterson. *Theater Careers: A Realistic Guide*. Columbia, SC: University of South Carolina Press, 2012.

Han, Yaya, Allison DeBlasio, and Joey Marsocci. *1,000 Incredible Costume & Cosplay Ideas: A Showcase of Creative Characters in Anime, Manga, Video Games, Movies, Comics, and More!* Minneapolis, MN: Rockport Publishers, 2013.

Mason, Helen. *Costume Designer*. New York, NY: Gareth Stevens Publishing, 2014.

Mass, AJ. *Yes, It's Hot in Here: Adventures in the Weird, Woolly, World of Sports Mascots*. New York, NY: Rodale, 2014.

Rooney, Anne. *Creative and Media Careers*. Mankato, MN: Amicus, 2011.

Savage, Steven, and Ellen Marlow. *Focused Fandom: Cosplay, Costuming, and Careers*. CreateSpace Publishing, 2013.

Staley, Erin. *A Career as an Event Coordinator*. New York, NY: Rosen Publishing, 2015.

Stearman, Kaye. *Travel and Tourism Careers*. Mankato, MN: Amicus, 2011.

Von Finn, Denny. *Roller Coasters*. Minneapolis, MN: Bellwether Media, 2010.

Wooster, Patricia. *So, You Want to Work in Fashion?: How to Break into the World of Fashion and Design*. New York, NY: Aladdin, 2014.

Belli, Mary Lou, and Dinah Lenney. *Acting for Young Actors*. New York, NY: Back Stage Books, 2006.

Bureau of Labor Statistics. "Occupational Employment and Wages, May 2014: 39-3091 Amusement and Recreation Attendants," May 2014. Retrieved April 20, 2015 (http://www.bls.gov/oes/current/oes393091 .htm).

Calaway Park. "Employment: Auditions." Retrieved April 25, 2015 (http:// www.calawaypark.com/audition.html).

Cedar Point. "Summer Jobs." Retrieved April 2, 2015 (https://www.cedarpoint .com/item/Jobs/Summer-Jobs).

Disney Careers. "Explore Our Stories." Retrieved April 2, 2015 (http:// disneycareers.com/en/working-here/explore-our-stories).

Dorney Park. "Seasonal Positions." Retrieved May 9, 2015 (https:// www.dorneypark.com/jobs/seasonal-positions).

Duncan, David. Former Disney employee. Interview with the author, May 3, 2015.

Knott's Berry Farm. "Special Events Openings." Retrieved April 2, 2015 (https://www.knotts.com/jobs/special-events-openings).

Legoland Parks. "Entertainment Auditions." Retrieved May 4, 2015 (http://california.legoland.com/about_us/Entertainment-Department -Auditions).

Mandel, Peter. "A Day in the Life of a Theme Park Character." *Huffington Post*, July 13, 2013. Retrieved April 2, 2015 (http://www.huffingtonpost .com/peter-mandel/a-day-in-the-life-of-a-theme-park -character_b_1662884.html).

Rooney, Anne. *Creative and Media Careers*. Mankato, MN: Amicus, 2011.

Spitz, Jill Jorden. "For Theme-Park Characters, the Job Is No Costume Party." *Orlando Sentinel*, January 27, 1998. Retrieved April 2, 2015 (http:// community.seattletimes.nwsource.com/archive/?date=19980127 &slug=2730879).

Stearman, Kaye. *Travel and Tourism Careers*. Mankato, MN: Amicus, 2011.

Willett, Megan. "A Former 'Snow White' Dishes About Life as a Disney Park Princess. *Business Insider*, April 8, 2013. Retrieved April 24, 2015 (http:// www.businessinsider.com/former-disney-princess-tells-all-2013-4).

ABOUT THE AUTHOR

Bobi Martin is a published author of books, magazine pieces, and web copy. She has been to several of the theme parks and amusement parks mentioned in this book! She has acted and danced with a small community theater group and choreographed dance numbers for some productions.

PHOTO CREDITS